EMBRACE YOUR DREAMS

MY INGREDIENTS FOR SUCCESS

Annakay Hutchinson

EMBRACE YOUR DREAMS: MY INGREDIENTS FOR SUCCESS

Copyright © 2019 by Annakay Hutchinson

For more information about this author please visit https://forchangebebold.com

This eBook is licensed for your personal enjoyment only. This eBook may not be re-sold or given away to other people. If you would like to share this book with another person, then please return to amazon.com and purchase an additional copy.

All rights reserved. No part of this publication may be reproduced, distributed, or transmitted in any form or by any means, including photocopying, recording, or other electronic or mechanical methods, without the prior written permission of the publisher, except in the case of brief quotations embodied in critical reviews and certain other noncommercial uses permitted by copyright law.

Editing by The Pro Book Editor
Cover Design by Ayir.tech

ISBN: 9781696512633

Main category—Non-Fiction

CONTENTS

EMBRACE YOUR DREAMS

Contents

Introduction

Examine Your Life
   Change starts with you.

Shift into Drive
   Action brings results.

Embrace Your Fears
   Remember your dreams.

Shifting Lanes
   The harder you work, the greater the results!

Finding Your Voice
   Don't be afraid to seek help.

Making a Stop
   Don't stop before crossing the finish line!

Shaping Your Mindset (Vision and Goals)
   Your mind is powerful. What you put in will eventually start showing outwardly.

Protect Your Mindset
   Fuel your mindset with positivity.

Thank You, Readers!

About the Author

Embrace Your Dreams: My Ingredients for Success is a short book designed to get you ready to shift gears from park to drive. It's time you start living your dream life. The only way you can do that is to face head-on the fears you hold deep within. Take this journey with me and you will find that becoming an effective leader, business coach, business owner, or mentor first requires a commitment to start. Start moving, start building, start dreaming, start exploring, and eventually, you will see your dreams become reality.

–Annakay

INTRODUCTION

One of my goals in life is to help as many people as I can to identify their true passion and purpose. I grew up hearing the phrase "life is what you make it," which I've found to be very accurate throughout my life. You are in control of how you allow things to affect you physically, emotionally, and spiritually. Whether you want to sit in the situation you are in or rise above it is entirely up to you.

Do not for a second get me wrong. I know there are many people in this world wishing they could rise above their current status in life. It takes time to rise out of life's difficult challenges, and sometimes it takes help from others and being willing to seek out and accept that help, but it's possible to do so. Therefore, I am not here to tell anyone they are lazy or worthless, but rather, my objective is to share my understanding of success and the drive needed to push toward achieving it.

This book flourished after I completed an eight-day summer challenge called "Birth tha' Book" by Rosanne Reid in 2017. I had always wanted to write a book but felt my story would not be taken seriously, until 2017 when I looked back at my own life, my experiences, and the decision I had to make to be the person I wanted to become. You see, you can always look at the outward appearance of a person and believe you've got them all figured out, but it's not until you hear their story that your outlook changes completely.

So, this book will focus on the ingredients I have used to become an Entrepreneur, a Certified Goal Success Coach, and a Podcast Host while also staying spiritually grounded in my faith.

CHAPTER 1

EXAMINE YOUR LIFE

Change starts with you.

I read, I study, I examine, I listen, I think, and out of all that I try to form an idea into which I put as much common sense as I can.
–Marquis de Lafayette

You have probably heard this a million times growing up. "You can do anything you put your mind to." Well, at least to an extent, right? I don't want you going around doing illegal things. However, we are all capable of doing anything we wish to achieve. Today, if you decide to take a walk, then you will take a walk. If you choose to go for a run, then you will go for a run. Today, if you decide to be happy, then you will be happy!

One of the essential ingredients for success that we will focus on in this book is examining your life. When you start learning about who you are through the process called self-examination, you begin to understand your limits, strengths, and boundaries. Self-examination plays a crucial part in just about any area of study, business, adventure, and/or leadership role you might take on. Knowing who you are as an individual will help you maneuver your life better. Examination of one's self is tough and will not take place in just a day. Just recently, I did a self-examination on my life to understand my growth over the past year and, to tell you the truth, I have come a long way.

Take 15 minutes right now to examine your life using the following questions and prompts.

Please think about your purpose and write it down.

_____
_____
_____
_____
_____
_____

Think about where you were this time last year. Have you improved as an individual since then? If yes, in what way did you improve? If no, how can you improve over the year in front of you?

_____
_____
_____
_____
_____
_____

Did you improve on your spiritual relationship? If yes, in what way did you improve? If no, how can you improve over the year in front of you?

_____
_____
_____

_____
_____
_____

Did you make changes in how you view life?

_____
_____
_____
_____
_____
_____

Are you happy?

_____
_____
_____
_____
_____
_____

Are your current life choices helping you have a positive impact on others, your spouse, your children, or even in your own life?

_____
_____
_____
_____
_____

If your decision is to create a better life, a better experience for yourself and those around you, then start by examining your life. My self-examination hit me hard after attending a Success Conference back in 2016 with my father. The Success Conference is a yearly event highlighting success stories and achievements of business owners in the company. I was so excited to be part of the fantastic event and to be recognized by a great company amongst amazing mompreneurs, business coaches, and top leaders. Before the event ended, a couple from the Philippines stood to share their story as new business coaches and the struggles they had experienced. They explained that the language barrier was one of their biggest issues, so they were filled with so much fear when they first started, but they did not allow that to impede their growth. They instead put a lot of work into practicing their English while building their business, and within three months of being a part of the company, they were promoted.

Which brings me back to my opening quote. "You can do anything you put your mind to." That couple had a goal, and they did a self-examination that led them to understanding their weakness but didn't allow the barrier to stop their progress. Instead, they implemented grit and will power and made up their minds to accomplish the goal ahead. This made me realize that if they can do it, I can do it too. I drew from their grit, hosted webinars, attended different life-change conferences with top leaders, and did not for a second let anything stop me from sharing my own story. I will not make you think it was an easy road—it was hard—but it was all worth it.

CHAPTER 2

SHIFT INTO DRIVE

Action brings results.

Only new actions will bring different results.
—Billy Cox

The first thing you do before starting to drive is learn *how* to drive. I am sure we've all had many different teachers—maybe our parents, a driving school, a boyfriend, or our grandparents. The one thing that I am sure we all had in common was *practicing*. I recall Sunday evenings, and even after school, taking maybe 30-40 minutes to practice every chance I got. I used the DMV parking lot, school parking lot, and even my neighborhood as practice areas. As I improved, I ventured out to the major streets. The most important thing I did was to begin! Then that action led me to become more focused, more driven, and more determined.

I want you to think about that business idea and your personal life as learning how to drive. Before you can start building that brand or embracing your dreams, you need to learn the necessary techniques to start producing changes. Your business and your personal life will require the same attention, same time management that you put into learning how to drive.

I remember the very first time I sat in the driver's seat, how impatient I was. All I wanted was to get my license. I am sure you have been in my shoes. A funny thing happened to me after signing up for a lesson from a driving school. I had thought the experience was going to get me on the road, driving, so was excited and eager to start not knowing that the entire first lesson was about learning the different areas of a car. So now you can imagine how disappointed I was, but I still gained a fantastic lesson from that day. Be patient!

When you start to embrace your dreams, you have to learn how to be patient with yourself. Yes, I know that excited feeling to get the business idea off the ground, to complete your degree, to dream it and instantly achieve it, but if you're not fully prepared, you can cause more harm than good to yourself and others.

Within that one-hour driving lesson, I learned the different parts of a vehicle. If someone were to ask where the spare tire and jack are located for changing a flat, I would be able to answer without hesitation. Be patient with yourself! Getting the right tools and resources before leaping ahead will prevent this old saying from being true about you: "The blind leading the blind." So, do not be so eager to hop into the driver's seat without proper knowledge and understanding.

CHAPTER 3

EMBRACE YOUR FEARS

Remember your dreams.

With integrity, you have nothing to fear, since you have nothing to hide. With integrity, you will do the right thing so that you will have no guilt.

–Zig Ziglar

Marcus Aurelius said, "It's not the death that a man should fear, but he should fear never beginning to live." Fear is like a bacterium that spreads throughout the body if not adequately treated. It sneaks up when we least expect it and tries to put negative thoughts in our minds. How many times per day are you in constant war with yourself about doing something? Do thoughts like these rush through your mind?

I am not good enough!
What if they hate it?
I don't think I can!
What if they laugh at me?
I am too tired today!
Maybe tomorrow!

I don't know about any of you, but for me, these were a part of my life for a very long time. I found myself constantly worried about what others would say, how their reactions would be, before I did anything. I soon realized I was in complete fear of failure. I did not want to fail and so to avoid it, I found excuses not to breathe. I called fear a suffocater.

But, remember that through self-examination we can improve. Once I realized my fears were holding me back, I could change that. So, below you will find the ways I have used fear as a driving force in my life.

1). The first thing I did was create a list called Fears I Have.

It's the things we fear the most that will help us to take a leap of faith into the chapter of our lives that will be rewarding. Do not hesitate to list all your fears. Fears are not a failure; they help us be the best us. I started this exercise back in 2017, when I first started writing this book. It was one of the hardest things I have done because I had so many fears.

Here are some of my fears that I wrote down:

Public Speaking
Letting My Guard Down
AGE
Goal Setting
Hearing the word "NO"
Writing My Coaching Program

2). The second thing I did was work that list like a to-do list by completing something that required me to face each fear one by one.

In 2018, I crossed all these fears off my list. I have spoken in public, in person and live on Instagram. I have created my coaching package. I have eliminated the idea that age matters from my mind. And I have pushed past being scared of the concept of goal setting by making and completing many goals. Was it easy? Hell *no*! It was straight up incredibly difficult! It was gut crunching terrifying, but I pushed through. And I soon learned that the more I worked on concurring my fears, the more I felt at ease in tackling another. My confidence grew, and I was honestly happy that I hadn't allowed my fears to dominate my life anymore.

Create a list of your fears that have been holding you back. Set daily, weekly, and/or monthly goals for each item on your list. Then take the time to begin facing your fears and crossing them off your list one by one.

If you want to completely move your business and/or personal life into drive, you cannot allow fear to be a stumbling block to your growth. Instead, use it as a driving force.

Remember, fear stands for:

F - FALSE

E - EMOTIONS

A - APPEARING

R - REAL

Join the conversation on my Instagram @forchangebebold You can use #forchangebebold #dailyreminderwithannakay.

CHAPTER 4

SHIFTING LANES

The harder you work, the greater the results!

I had no choice but to Boss Up and Create my lane.
—MK Global

Now that you have established the groundwork and are making changes to improve your business and personal life, it's time to start considering shifting lanes. As a new driver, this can be one of the most terrifying things to do. However, since you have acquired the right amount of practice, you are now ready to take on any challenge. Do you stop learning after you receive your license? No! Continuous learning is how we continue to grow our skill sets.

When shifting from one lane to another, there could be an impact caused by impatience. It happens. You will find that as soon as you're confident in who you are or what you do, something happens to create the fear you have just gotten over. You might ask yourself these questions:

Was I ready?

Is it safe to make this move at this moment? Alternatively, is it safe to make this deal?

The change can be useful for business or personal life choices. What you will never know is whether a change will be good or bad if you never try.

CHAPTER 5

FINDING YOUR VOICE

Don't be afraid to seek help.

It took me quite a long time to develop a voice, and now that I have it, I am not going to be silent.
–Madeleine Albright

When you shift lanes, it can be tough to navigate if you have someone else hovering over your every move. Can you recall driving your parents while they constantly told you what to do? Doesn't it cause more of a distraction than anything else? Well, when you shift lanes, you will have business partners, family members, and even friends adding their suggestions to the movement.

Let's be clear, I'm not saying you shouldn't listen to your business partners or family members or friends for advice. What I am saying is that when you lose control over your vehicle, you can swerve into another lane instead of smoothly transitioning over. Speak up for what you want and need to learn and grow in your life journey. Don't be pushed or pulled into decisions or actions that you aren't prepared for yet.

Finding your voice takes time—do not rush it. Many of the most influential people are still finding their voices. Never speed the process of becoming who you want to be—instead, incorporate habits that position you to continuously grow. Then take it one step at a time. It's important to understand where you stand in your business, as much as it's essential to use your voice to allow people around you to know what you stand for.

CHAPTER 6

MAKING A STOP

Don't stop before crossing the finish line!

Never rest on your laurels. Never Quit. Never stop working to make the world a better place. That's our unfinished business.
–Hillary Clinton

You've got everything under control. You're starting to overcome the fears you had been holding onto and have started the brainstorming process for your success. There is always a time when a vehicle must come to a stop, whether it be at a red light, a stop sign, or even an accident. Just like a vehicle, we will sometimes need to come to a stop with our planning and/or our progress. This stop does not mean we have quit or are giving up. It simply means we need to be reminded of our journey, the "why." Don't get distracted during the stop. Wait to make your next move and keep driving toward that goal. Yes, you might find some struggles along the way, but the important thing is to keep focus.

Capitalize on coaches, accountability partners, those who will help you shift from the mini-stop, back into drive. Many times, we get to a stop without realizing that it's okay.

Yes, it's okay to stop!

It's okay to revisit your "Why."

It's okay to get some help.

The following chapters will help remind you of your "Why" and what you need to become a successful person and never come to a permanent stop in your life.

CHAPTER 7

SHAPING YOUR MINDSET (VISION AND GOALS)

Your mind is powerful. What you put in will eventually start showing outwardly.

Growth hacking is a mindset, and those who have it will reap incredible gains.

–Ryan Holiday

Developing the right mindset is crucial to succeeding in anything. When I started my business back in 2015, I knew I had to change my mindset by creating a process that not only empowered me but gives me the confidence I needed to succeed. So, I kept reading, educating myself in the field of business, listened to successful business coaches, and attended meetings to better empower myself while staying focused on the mission I had set out to accomplish.

So, what exactly is a Mindset?

Mindset is a fixed mental attitude or disposition that predetermines a person's responses to and interpretations of situations. Think of it as an inclination, or habit. It's your understanding of who you are, what your beliefs are, and who those surrounding you are. And it determines how you will react to information and situations.

Creating a mindset shaped with vision and goals requires a positive attitude and belief that you can change your mindset. You might be thinking this is easier said than done, but with commitment and daily discipline, it's possible to create a positive mindset with vision and goals. Vision and goals are necessary tools for any professional business owner, student, and just about anyone in the working world. It's essential to have vision and goals that work hand in hand, paving the way for you and keeping you on track.

When you have vision and goals, you can keep focused on your plans and push through all the obstacles, making them a reality. I completed so many goals in the process of creating more visions and goals! Don't just stop at one—move on to making more. Have fun, embrace your dreams, embrace your passions, embrace the true you. Don't be afraid to explore new things. Don't be scared to challenge yourself. Challenge makes you stronger, wiser, and smarter. Empower yourself to do more, to go beyond your comfort zone, and break free of your fears.

WRITE DOWN YOUR GOALS

CREATE A VISION BOARD

Materials Needed (Walmart, Dollar Store, Michaels)

**Tri-fold board

**Glue/Tape

**Newspaper

**Magazines

**Images off the internet

"Dreams without goals are just dreams. Dreams without goals require discipline and consistency." –Denzel Washington.

CHAPTER 8

PROTECT YOUR MINDSET

Fuel your mindset with positivity.

To create something exceptional, your mindset must be relentlessly focused on the smallest detail.
–Giorgio Armani

One of the most important things you can do is create a daily mindset routine. The goal of the routine is to continually feed your mind with only positive and uplifting information that will help you keep performing at your best. Everyday life challenges have a way of creating a wave of negativity that prevents you from performing at your highest throughout the day.

Here are three ways to protect your mindset:

1) Rise Early

Rising early enhances your chances of succeeding. Have you ever heard the saying, "Early birds catch the most worms?" If you rise late, you will always be rushing. When you rise early, you can get everything done without the pressure of having to rush. Rising early gives you the chance to listen to a podcast, meditate, pray, and read your bible. My daily routine consists of reading my bible, praying, sharing a #dailyreminderwithannakay on my Instagram page, and meditating on the positivity of my day. I try not to dwell on negativity, though it sure does come up every now and then. But I reinforce my mindset with a positive song, quote, or a verse from the bible to keep my day positive.

2) Read Positive Books

Reading positive and informative books will help you strengthen your mindset while educating your mind. Taking advice from others who have been in the same situation as you and seeing how they overcome can help you navigate. Here are three incredible books and podcast that you should read/listen to:

Make It Count: Tips on Unlocking Your Vision by Nicole McLaren Campbell

Get Over Your Damn Self: The No-BS Blueprint to Building a Life-Changing Business by Romi Neustadt

One Happy Thought at a Time: 30 Days to a Happier You by Rochelle Gapere

The Network Marketing Mum with Emma Cooper (podcast)

For Change Be Bold with Annakay Hutchinson (podcast)

3) Engage in Positive Conversation

Find the right people and the proper conversations to help you protect your mindset. It's important to feed your mind with positive words and interactions daily as the more you live by a positive mindset, the more you start to live your dream life.

Thank You, Readers!

Thanks for taking this journey with me. I want each and every one of you to know that it is your time. Find your voice. Find the right moment and begin your journey. You are never too old, never too young, and will never be too late to start creating change and impacting lives. You might not feel the need to start today nor see why it's such an important task, but your movement can create an effective change for someone else who looks at life the same way you do. I challenge you to shift into drive. I challenge you to shift into another lane. And I challenge you to never come to a permanent stop!

About the Author

Annakay Hutchinson is a Health Care Major, Network Business Coach, Certified Goal Success Coach, and Entrepreneur known for always smiling, always uplifting, and being devoted to making sure she impacts change in the life of others. She has an old soul and has mastered being happy and embracing her dreams and goals. The release of her first book, *EMBRACE YOUR DREAMS: MY INGREDIENTS FOR SUCCESS*, has just added more fuel to the burning fire lit many years ago. Sharing her understanding on social media, with close friends, with business partners, and more are just a few ways Annakay helps individuals realize their potential.

Happiness is your birthright!

If you would like to work with Annakay Hutchinson one to one or in a group setting, please contact her:

Instagram: @iamannakayhutchinson

Twitter: @Annakaybusiness

Email: annakayhutchinson@gmail.com

Annakay is committed to you if you are committed to seeing results!

www.ingramcontent.com/pod-product-compliance
Lightning Source LLC
Chambersburg PA
CBHW040301220526
45473CB00002B/552